I0500547

War Powers Resolution:
Presidential Compliance

Richard F. Grimmett
Specialist in International Security

September 25, 2012

Congressional Research Service

7-5700

www.crs.gov

RL33532

CRS Report for Congress ───────────────────

Prepared for Members and Committees of Congress

Summary

Two separate but closely related issues confront Congress each time the President introduces Armed Forces into a situation abroad that conceivably could lead to their involvement in hostilities. One issue concerns the division of war powers between the President and Congress, whether the use of Armed Forces falls within the purview of the congressional power to declare war and the War Powers Resolution (WPR). The other issue is whether or not Congress concurs in the wisdom of the action. This report does not deal with the substantive merits of using Armed Forces in specific cases, but rather with congressional authorization for military action, and the application and effectiveness of the WPR. The purpose of the WPR (P.L. 93-148, passed over President Nixon's veto on November 7, 1973) is to ensure that Congress and the President share in making decisions that may get the United States involved in hostilities. Compliance becomes an issue whenever the President introduces U.S. forces abroad in situations that might be construed as hostilities or imminent hostilities. Criteria for compliance include prior consultation with Congress, fulfillment of the reporting requirements, and congressional authorization. If the President has not complied fully, the issue becomes what action Congress should take to bring about compliance or to influence U.S. policy. A related issue has been congressional authorization of U.N. peacekeeping or other U.N.-sponsored actions.

For over three decades, war powers and the War Powers Resolution have been an issue in U.S. military actions in Asia, the Middle East, Africa, Central America, and Europe. Presidents have submitted 136 reports to Congress as a result of the War Powers Resolution, although only one (the Mayaguez situation) cited Section 4(a)(1) or specifically stated that forces had been introduced into hostilities or imminent hostilities. Congress invoked the WPR in the Multinational Force in Lebanon Resolution (P.L. 98-119), which authorized the Marines to remain in Lebanon for 18 months. In addition, P.L. 102-1, enacted in January 1991, authorizing the use of U.S. Armed Forces in response to Iraqi aggression against Kuwait, stated that it constituted specific statutory authorization within the meaning of the WPR. On November 9, 1993, the House used a section of the WPR to state that U.S. forces should be withdrawn from Somalia by March 31, 1994; Congress had already taken this action in appropriations legislation. War powers have been at issue in former Yugoslavia/Bosnia/Kosovo, Iraq, and Haiti. Authorizing military actions in response to the terrorist attacks against the United States of September 11, 2001, through P.L. 107-40 directly involved war powers. The continued use of force to obtain Iraqi compliance with U.N. resolutions remained a war powers issue from the end of the Gulf War on February 28, 1991, until the enactment of P.L. 107-243 in October 2002, which explicitly authorized the President to use force against Iraq, an authority he exercised in March 2003, and continues to exercise for military operations in Iraq. Most recently, issues associated with presidential compliance with the War Powers Resolution have arisen over his use of U.S. military forces to support a U.N. sanctioned "no-fly zone" in Libya, without obtaining congressional authorization for such action.

Debate continues on whether using the War Powers Resolution is effective as a means of assuring congressional participation in decisions that might get the United States involved in a significant military conflict. Proposals have been made to modify or repeal the resolution. None have been enacted to date. This report will be updated as events warrant.

Contents

Contacts

Most Recent Developments

On September 14, 2012, the President reported to Congress, "consistent with" the War Powers Resolution, that on September 12, 2012, he ordered deployed to Libya "a security force from the U.S. Africa Command" to "support the security of U.S. personnel in Libya." This action was taken in response to the attack on the U.S. "diplomatic post in Benghazi, Libya" that had killed four America citizens, including U.S. Ambassador John Christopher Stevens. The President added on September 13, 2012, that "an additional security force arrived in Yemen in response to security threats there." He further stated that: "Although these security forces are equipped for combat, these movements have been undertaken solely for the purpose of protecting American citizens and property." These security forces will remain in Libya and in Yemen, he noted, "until the security situation becomes such that they are no longer needed."

On June 15, 2012, President reported to Congress "consistent with" the War Powers Resolution, a consolidated report regarding various deployments of U.S. Armed Forces equipped for combat. In the efforts in support of U.S. counterterrorism (CT) objectives against al-Qa'ida, the Taliban, and associated forces, he noted that U.S. forces were engaged in Afghanistan in the above effort were "approximately 90,000." With regard to other counter-terrorism operations, the President stated that the United States had deployed "U.S. combat-equipped forces to assist in enhancing the CT capabilities of our friends and allies including special operations and other forces for sensitive operations in various locations around the world. He noted that the "U.S. military has taken direct action in Somalia against members of al-Qa'ida, including those who are also members of al-Shabaab, who are engaged in efforts to carry out terrorist attacks against the United States and our interests." The President further stated that the U.S. military had been "working closely with the Yemini government to operationally and ultimately eliminate the terrorist threat posed by al-Qaida in the Arabian Peninsula (AQAP), the most active and dangerous affiliate of al-Qa'ida today." He added that these "joint efforts have resulted in direct action against a limited number of AQAP operatives and senior leaders in that country who posed a terrorist threat to the United States and our interests." The President noted that he would direct "additional measures against al-Qa'ida, the Taliban, and associated forces to protect U.S. citizens and interests." Further information on such matters is provided in a "classified annex to this report."

Other military operations reported by the President include the deployment of U.S. combat-equipped military personnel to Uganda "to serve as advisors to regional forces that are working to apprehend or remove Joseph Kony and other senior Lord's Resistance Army (LRA) leaders from the battlefield and to protect local populations." The total number of U.S. military personnel deployed for this mission is "approximately 90," and elements of these U.S. forces have been sent to "forward locations in the LRA-affected areas of the Republic of South Sudan, the Democratic Republic of the Congo, and the Central African Republic." These U.S. forces "will not engage LRA forces except in self-defense."

The President also reported that presently the United States was contributing "approximately 817 military personnel: to the NATO-led Kosovo Force (KFOR) in Kosovo." He also reported that the United States remained prepared to engage in "maritime interception operations" intended to stop the "movement, arming, and financing of certain international terrorist groups," as well as stopping "proliferation by sea of weapons of mass destruction and related materials." Additional details about these efforts are included in "the classified annex" to the President's report.

Background and Analysis

Under the Constitution, war powers are divided. Congress has the power to declare war and raise and support the Armed Forces (Article I, Section 8), while the President is Commander in Chief (Article II, Section 2). It is generally agreed that the Commander in Chief role gives the President power to repel attacks against the United States and makes him responsible for leading the Armed Forces. During the Korean and Vietnam wars, the United States found itself involved for many years in undeclared wars. Many Members of Congress became concerned with the erosion of congressional authority to decide when the United States should become involved in a war or the use of Armed Forces that might lead to war. On November 7, 1973, Congress passed the War Powers Resolution (P.L. 93-148) over the veto of President Nixon.

The War Powers Resolution (WPR) states that the President's powers as Commander in Chief to introduce U.S. forces into hostilities or imminent hostilities are exercised only pursuant to (1) a declaration of war; (2) specific statutory authorization; or (3) a national emergency created by an attack on the United States or its forces. It requires the President in every possible instance to consult with Congress before introducing American Armed Forces into hostilities or imminent hostilities unless there has been a declaration of war or other specific congressional authorization. It also requires the President to report to Congress any introduction of forces into hostilities or imminent hostilities, Section 4(a)(1); into foreign territory while equipped for combat, Section 4(a)(2); or in numbers which substantially enlarge U.S. forces equipped for combat already in a foreign nation, Section 4(a)(3). Once a report is submitted "or required to be submitted" under Section 4(a)(1), Congress must authorize the use of forces within 60 to 90 days or the forces must be withdrawn. (For detailed background, see CRS Report R41199, *The War Powers Resolution: After Thirty-Six Years*, by Richard F. Grimmett, and CRS Report RL31133, *Declarations of War and Authorizations for the Use of Military Force: Historical Background and Legal Implications*, by Jennifer K. Elsea and Richard F. Grimmett.) It is important to note that since the War Powers Resolution's enactment over President Nixon's veto in 1973, every President has taken the position that it is an unconstitutional infringement by Congress on the President's authority as Commander in Chief. The courts have not directly addressed this question.

United Nations Actions

U.N. Security Council resolutions provide authority for U.S. action under international law. Whether congressional authorization is required under domestic law depends on the types of U.N. action and is governed by the Constitution and the U.N. Participation Act (P.L. 79-264, as amended), as well as by the War Powers Resolution. Section 8(b) of the War Powers Resolution exempts only participation in headquarters operations of joint military commands established prior to 1973.

For armed actions under Articles 42 and 43 of the U.N. Charter, Section 6 of the U.N. Participation Act authorizes the President to negotiate special agreements with the Security Council, subject to the approval of Congress, providing for the numbers and types of Armed Forces and facilities to be made available to the Security Council. Once the agreements have been concluded, further congressional authorization is not necessary, but no such agreements have been concluded. Some Members have sought to encourage negotiation of military agreements under Article 43 of the U.N. Charter. Questions include whether congressional approval is required only for an initial agreement on providing peacekeeping forces in general, or for each agreement to provide forces in specific situations, and how such approvals would relate to the War Powers Resolution.

Section 7 of the U.N. Participation Act authorizes the detail of up to 1,000 personnel to serve in any noncombatant capacity for certain U.N. peaceful settlement activities. The United States has provided personnel to several U.N. peacekeeping missions, such as observers to the U.N. Truce Supervision Organization in Palestine. In these instances, controversy over the need for congressional authorization has not occurred because the action appeared to fall within the authorization in Section 7 of the Participation Act. Controversy has arisen when forces have been deployed in larger numbers or as possible combatants.

In the 103rd Congress, Members used several vehicles in seeking some control over future peacekeeping actions wherever they might occur. Both the Defense Appropriations Act for FY1994, P.L. 103-139 (§8153), and for FY1995, P.L. 103-335 (§8103), stated the sense of Congress that funds should not be used for U.N. peacekeeping or peace enforcement operations unless the President consulted with Congress at least 15 days in advance whenever possible. Section 1502 of the Defense Authorization for FY1994, P.L. 103-160, required the President to submit by April 1, 1994, a report on multinational peacekeeping including the requirement of congressional approval for participation and the applicability of the War Powers Resolution and the U.N. Participation Act.

Along similar lines, the conference report accompanying the Department of State Appropriations Act for FY1994, H.R. 2519 (P.L. 103-121, signed October 27, 1993), called for the Secretary of State to notify both Appropriations Committees 15 days in advance, where practicable, of a vote by the U.N. Security Council to establish any new or expanded peacekeeping mission. The Foreign Relations Authorization Act, P.L. 103-236, signed April 30, 1994, established new requirements for consultation with Congress on U.S. participation in U.N. peacekeeping operations. Section 407 required monthly consultations on the status of peacekeeping operations and advance reports on resolutions that would authorize a new U.N. peacekeeping operation. It also required 15 days' advance notice of any U.S. assistance to support U.N. peacekeeping operations and a quarterly report on all assistance that had been provided to the U.N. for peacekeeping operations. To permit presidential flexibility, conferees explained, the quarterly report need not include temporary duty assignments of U.S. personnel in support of peacekeeping operations of less than 20 personnel in any one case.

The following discussion provides background on major cases of U.S. military involvement in overseas operations in recent years that have raised War Powers questions.

Former Yugoslavia/Bosnia

The issue of war powers and whether congressional authorization is necessary for U.S. participation in U.N. action was also raised by efforts to halt fighting in the former territory of Yugoslavia, particularly in Bosnia. The United States participated without congressional authorization in airlifts into Sarajevo, naval monitoring of sanctions, aerial enforcement of a "no-fly zone," and aerial enforcement of safe havens.

Because some of the U.S. action has been taken within a NATO framework, action in Bosnia has raised the broader issue of whether action under NATO is exempt from the requirements of the War Powers Resolution or its standard for the exercise of war powers under the Constitution.

Article 11 of the North Atlantic Treaty states that its provisions are to be carried out by the parties "in accordance with their respective constitutional processes," implying some role for Congress in the event of war. Section 8(a) of the War Powers Resolution states that authority to introduce U.S. forces into hostilities is not to be inferred from any treaty, ratified before or after 1973, unless implementing legislation specifically authorizes such introduction and says it is intended to constitute an authorization within the meaning of the War Powers Resolution. Section 8(b) states that nothing in the Resolution should be construed to require further authorization for U.S. participation in the headquarters operations of military commands established before 1973, such as NATO headquarters operations.

On August 13, 1992, the U.N. Security Council adopted Resolution 770 calling on all nations to take "all measures necessary" to facilitate the delivery of humanitarian assistance to Sarajevo. On August 11, 1992, the Senate passed S.Res. 330 urging the President to work for such a resolution and pledging funds for participation, but saying that no U.S. military personnel should be introduced into hostilities without clearly defined objectives. On the same day, the House passed H.Res. 554 urging the Security Council to authorize measures, including the use of force, to ensure humanitarian relief. Thus, both chambers of Congress supported action but not by legislation authorizing the use of U.S. forces. For details of congressional actions relating to Bosnia from 1993 through 1995, see CRS Report R41199, *The War Powers Resolution: After Thirty-Six Years*, by Richard F. Grimmett.

In late 1995, the issue of war powers and Bosnia was raised again as President Clinton sent more than 20,000 American combat troops to Bosnia as part of a NATO-led peacekeeping force. In December 1995, Congress considered and voted on a number of bills and resolutions, but the House and Senate could not come to consensus on any single measure. Subsequently, President Clinton in December 1996 agreed to provide up to 8,500 ground troops to participate in a NATO-led follow-on force in Bosnia termed the Stabilization Force (SFOR). On March 18, 1998, the House defeated by a vote of 193-225, H.Con.Res. 227, a resolution directing the President, pursuant to Section 5(c) of the War Powers Resolution, to remove United States Armed Forces from the Republic of Bosnia and Herzegovina (H.Rept. 105-442). (For additional information, see CRS Report RL32392, *Bosnia and Herzegovina: Issues for U.S. Policy*, by Steven Woehrel; CRS Report RL32282, *Bosnia and Kosovo: U.S. Military Operations*, by Steve Bowman; and CRS Report R41199, *The War Powers Resolution: After Thirty-Six Years*, by Richard F. Grimmett.)

Kosovo

The issue of presidential authority to deploy forces in the absence of congressional authorization, under the War Powers Resolution, or otherwise, became an issue of significant controversy in late March 1999 when President Clinton ordered U.S. military forces to participate in a NATO-led military operation in Kosovo. This action has become the focus of an ongoing policy debate over the purpose and scope of U.S. military involvement in Kosovo. The President's action to commit forces to the NATO Kosovo operation also led to a suit in Federal District Court for the District of Columbia by some Members of Congress seeking a judicial finding that the President was violating the War Powers Resolution and the Constitution by using military forces in Yugoslavia in the absence of authorization from the Congress.

The Kosovo controversy began in earnest when on March 26, 1999, President Clinton notified the Congress "consistent with the War Powers Resolution," that on March 24, 1999, U.S. military forces, at his direction and in coalition with NATO allies, had commenced air strikes against

Yugoslavia in response to the Yugoslav government's campaign of violence and repression against the ethnic Albanian population in Kosovo. Prior to the President's action, the Senate, on March 23, 1999, had passed, by a vote of 58-41, S.Con.Res. 21, a nonbinding resolution expressing the sense of the Congress that the President was authorized to conduct "military air operations and missile strikes in cooperation with our NATO allies against the Federal Republic of Yugoslavia (Serbia and Montenegro)."

Subsequently, the House voted on a number of measures relating to U.S. participation in the NATO operation in Kosovo. On April 28, 1999, the House of Representatives passed H.R. 1569, by a vote of 249-180. This bill would prohibit the use of funds appropriated to the Defense Department from being used for the deployment of "ground elements" of the U.S. Armed Forces in the Federal Republic of Yugoslavia unless that deployment is specifically authorized by law. On that same day the House defeated H.Con.Res. 82, by a vote of 139-290. This resolution would have directed the President, pursuant to Section 5(c) of the War Powers Resolution, to remove U.S. Armed Forces from their positions in connection with the present operations against the Federal Republic of Yugoslavia. On April 28, 1999, the House also defeated H.J.Res. 44, by a vote of 2-427. This joint resolution would have declared a state of war between the United States and the "Government of the Federal Republic of Yugoslavia." The House on that same day also defeated, on a 213-213 tie vote, S.Con.Res. 21, the Senate resolution passed on March 23, 1999, that supported military air operations and missile strikes against Yugoslavia. On April 30, 1999, Representative Tom Campbell and 17 other Members of the House filed suit in Federal District Court for the District of Columbia seeking a ruling requiring the President to obtain authorization from Congress before continuing the air war, or taking other military action against Yugoslavia.

The Senate, on May 4, 1999, by a vote of 78-22, tabled S.J.Res. 20, a joint resolution, sponsored by Senator John McCain, that would authorize the President "to use all necessary force and other means, in concert with United States allies, to accomplish United States and North Atlantic Treaty Organization objectives in the Federal Republic of Yugoslavia (Serbia and Montenegro)." The House, meanwhile, on May 6, 1999, by a vote of 117-301, defeated an amendment by Representative Istook to H.R. 1664, the FY1999 defense supplemental appropriations bill, that would have prohibited the expenditure of funds in the bill to implement any plan to use U.S. ground forces to invade Yugoslavia, except in time of war. Congress, meanwhile, on May 20, 1999, cleared for the President's signature H.R. 1141, an emergency supplemental appropriations bill for FY1999, that provided billions in funding for the existing U.S. Kosovo operation.

On May 25, 1999, the 60th day had passed since the President notified Congress of his actions regarding U.S. participation in military operations in Kosovo. Representative Campbell, and those who joined his suit, noted to the Federal Court that this was a clear violation of the language of the War Powers Resolution stipulating a withdrawal of U.S. forces from the area of hostilities occur after 60 days in the absence of congressional authorization to continue, or a presidential request to Congress for an extra 30-day period to safely withdraw. The President did not seek such a 30-day extension, noting instead that the War Powers Resolution is constitutionally defective. On June 8, 1999, Federal District Judge Paul L. Friedman dismissed the suit of Representative Campbell and others that sought to have the court rule that President Clinton was in violation of the War Powers Resolution and the Constitution by conducting military activities in Yugoslavia without having received prior authorization from Congress. The judge ruled that Representative Campbell and others lacked legal standing to bring the suit (*Campbell v. Clinton*, 52 F. Supp. 2d 34 (D.D.C. 1999)). Representative Campbell appealed the ruling on June 24, 1999, to the U.S. Court of Appeals for the District of Columbia. The appeals court agreed to hear the case. On February 18, 2000, the appeals court affirmed the opinion of the

District Court that Representative Campbell and his co-plaintiffs lacked standing to sue the President. (Campbell v. Clinton, 203 F.3d 19 (D.C. Cir. 2000)). On May 18, 2000, Representative Campbell and 30 other Members of Congress appealed this decision to the United States Supreme Court. On October 2, 2000, the United States Supreme Court, without comment, refused to hear the appeal of Representative Campbell thereby letting stand the holding of the U.S. Court of Appeals. (Campbell v. Clinton, *cert. denied*, 531U.S. 815 October 2, 2000). On May 18, 2000, the Senate defeated, by a vote of 47-53, an amendment to S. 2521, the Senate's version of the Military Construction Appropriations Act, FY2001, that would have, among other things, terminated funding for the continued deployment of U.S. ground combat troops in Kosovo after July 1, 2001, unless the President sought and received congressional authorization to keep U.S. troops in Kosovo. (For detailed discussion of major issues, see CRS Report RL31053, *Kosovo and U.S. Policy: Background to Independence*, by Julie Kim and Steven Woehrel, and CRS Report RL30352, *War Powers Litigation Initiated by Members of Congress Since the Enactment of the War Powers Resolution*, by Michael John Garcia.)

Iraq: Post 1991

During the week of October 3, 1994, Iraq began sending two additional divisions to join regular forces in southern Iraq, close to the border of Kuwait. On October 8, President Clinton responded by sending about 30,000 additional U.S. forces and additional combat planes to join the forces already in the Gulf area. He said the United States would honor its commitment to defend Kuwait and enforce U.N. resolutions on Iraq. Congress recessed on October 8 until November 29, 1994, so it did not discuss the issue of congressional authorization. On October 28, President Clinton reported to Congress that by October 15 there were clear indications that Iraq had redeployed its forces to their original location. On November 7, the Defense Department announced 7,000 of the U.S. forces would be withdrawn before Christmas.

Earlier, three continuing situations in Iraq since the end of Desert Storm brought about the use of U.S. forces and thus raised war powers issues. The first situation resulted from the Iraqi government's repression of Kurdish and Shiite groups. U.N. Security Council Resolution 688 of April 5, 1991, condemned the repression of the Iraqi civilian population and appealed for contributions to humanitarian relief efforts. The second situation stemmed from the U.N. cease-fire resolution of April 3, 1991, Security Council Resolution 687, which called for Iraq to accept the destruction or removal of chemical and biological weapons, and international control of its nuclear materials.

The third situation was related to both of the earlier ones. On August 26, 1992, the United States, Britain, and France began a "no-fly" zone, banning Iraqi fixed wing and helicopter flights south of the 32nd parallel and creating a limited security zone in the south, where Shiite groups are concentrated. After violations of the no-fly zones and various other actions by Iraq, on January 13, 1993, the outgoing Bush Administration announced that aircraft from the United States and coalition partners had attacked missile bases in southern Iraq and that the United States was deploying a battalion task force to Kuwait to underline the United States' continuing commitment to Kuwait's independence. On January 6, 1993, the United States gave Iraq an ultimatum to remove newly deployed missiles in the no-fly zone. On January 19, 1993, President George H. W. Bush reported to Congress that U.S. aircraft on December 27, 1992, had shot down an Iraqi aircraft that had entered the no-fly zone and had undertaken further military actions on January 13, 17, and 18.

President Clinton said on January 21, 1993, that the United States would adhere to the policy toward Iraq set by the former Bush Administration, and on January 22, 23, April 9 and 18, June 19, and August 19, 1993, U.S. aircraft fired at targets in Iraq after pilots detected Iraqi radar or anti-aircraft fire directed at them. A number of such incidents occurred while planes patrolled the no-fly zone. On June 6, 1994, President Clinton reported that over the previous two years, the northern no-fly zone had deterred Iraq from a military offensive in the northern zone. Iraqi forces had responded to the no-fly zone in the south, he reported, by continuing to use land-based artillery to shell marsh villages. In addition, Iraq was conducting a large search and destroy operation and razing and burning marsh villages, in violation of U.N. Security Council Resolution 688. Until Iraq fully complied with all relevant U.N. Security Council resolutions, he reported, the United States would maintain sanctions and other measures designed to achieve compliance.

A war powers issue for years was whether the use of U.S. force in Iraq in the period after the early 1991 Desert Storm conflict had been authorized by Congress. P.L. 102-1 authorized the President to use U.S. Armed Forces pursuant to U.N. Security Council Resolution 678 to achieve implementation of previous Security Council Resolutions; Security Council Resolution 687 was adopted after this. On August 2, 1991, the Senate adopted an amendment to the Defense Authorization bill for FY1992 supporting the use of all necessary means to achieve the goals of Resolution 687. Senator Dole said the amendment was not intended to authorize the use of force by the President, and that in his view in the current circumstances the President required no specific authorization from Congress. As enacted, Section 1095 of P.L. 102-190 states the sense of Congress that it supports the use of all necessary means to achieve the goals of Security Council Resolution 687 as being consistent with the Authorization for Use of Military Force Against Iraq Resolution. The bill (§1096) also included an amendment by Senator Pell supporting the use of all necessary means to protect Iraq's Kurdish minority, consistent with relevant U.N. resolutions and authorities contained in P.L. 102-1.

In addition to these continuing situations, on June 28, 1993, President Clinton reported to Congress that on June 26, U.S. naval forces had launched a Tomahawk cruise missile strike on the Iraqi Intelligence Service's main command and control complex in Baghdad and that the military action was completed. He said the Iraqi Intelligence Service had planned the failed attempt to assassinate former President Bush during his visit to Kuwait in April 1993. On September 5, 1996, President Clinton reported to Congress on U.S. military actions in Iraq to obtain compliance with U.N. Security Council Resolutions, especially in light of attacks by Iraqi military forces against the Kurdish-controlled city of Irbil. U.S. actions ordered by the President included extending the no-fly zone in southern Iraq from 32 to 33 degrees north latitude, and cruise missile attacks from B-52H bombers and ships in the USS Carl Vinson Battle Group against fixed, surface-to-air missile sites, command and control centers, and air defense control facilities south of the 33rd parallel in Iraq. Except for the report of June 28, 1993, Presidents Bush and Clinton did not cite the War Powers Resolution in their reports related to military activities in Iraq in the period after the 1991 Gulf War. Rather, they submitted them "consistent with" P.L. 102-1, which required the President to submit a report to the Congress at least once every 60 days on the status of efforts to obtain compliance by Iraq with the U.N. Security Council resolution adopted in response to the Iraq aggression.

Starting in 1998 and through the end of the Clinton Administration, Iraq's refusal to permit U.N. weapons inspection teams access to various Iraqi sites, and Iraqi threats to U.S. aircraft policing the "no-fly zones" resulted in U.S. military action on numerous occasions against Iraqi military forces and targets in the "no-fly zones." President Clinton chose to report these actions under the requirements of P.L. 102-1, rather than the War Powers Resolution. In early February 2001,

President George W. Bush authorized U.S. aircraft to attack Iraqi radar installations in southern Iraq believed to threaten allied forces enforcing the "no-fly zone." Additional bombings of Iraqi sites were authorized and took place from the summer of 2001 into March 2003. Such actions, in the past, were reported under P.L. 102-1. Congress provided authorization for future military action, under specified conditions, through passage of P.L. 107-243 signed into law on October 16, 2002. In a report to Congress on January 20, 2003, pursuant to P.L. 107-243, President Bush stated that information required to be reported regarding actions taken against Iraq required by Section 3 of P.L. 102-1 would in the future be included in the reports required by P.L. 107-243. On March 19, 2003, President Bush directed U.S. Armed Forces to commence combat operations against Iraq to enforce its disarmament. Since he announced the end of major combat operations against Iraq on May 1, 2003, the President has made periodic reports on the current situation in Iraq "consistent with" P.L. 107-243, which have become the equivalent of reports to Congress envisioned by the War Powers Resolution. For a recent example of these reports to Congress see House Document 108-231, 108th Congress, 2nd session, submitted November 4, 2004. (For related information, see CRS Report RL31701, *Iraq: U.S. Military Operations*, by Steve Bowman, and CRS Report RL31339, *Iraq: Post-Saddam Governance and Security*, by Kenneth Katzman.)

Haiti

On July 3, 1993, Haitian military leader Raoul Cedras and deposed President Jean-Bertrand Aristide signed an agreement at Governors Island providing for the restoration of President Aristide on October 30. The United Nations and Organization of American States took responsibility for verifying compliance. Because the Haitian authorities did not comply with the agreement, on October 13, 1993, the U.N. Security Council voted to restore sanctions against Haiti. On October 20, President Clinton submitted a report "consistent with the War Powers Resolution" that U.S. ships had begun to enforce a U.N. embargo. Some Members of Congress complained that Congress had not been consulted about nor authorized the action. On October 18, 1993, Senator Dole said he would offer an amendment to the FY1994 Defense Appropriations bill (H.R. 3116) which would require congressional authorization for all deployments into Haitian waters and airspace unless the President made specified certifications. Congressional leaders and Administration officials negotiated the terms of the amendment. As enacted, Section 8147 of P.L. 103-139 stated the sense that funds should not be obligated or expended for U.S. military operations in Haiti unless the operations were (1) authorized in advance by Congress, (2) necessary to protect or evacuate U.S. citizens, (3) vital to the national security and there was not sufficient time to receive congressional authorization, or (4) the President submitted a report in advance that the intended deployment met certain criteria.

On May 6, 1994, the U.N. Security Council adopted Resolution 917 calling for measures to tighten the embargo. On June 10, 1994, President Clinton announced steps being taken to intensify the pressure on Haiti's military leaders that included assisting the Dominican Republic to seal its border with Haiti, using U.S. naval patrol boats to detain ships suspected of violating the sanctions, a ban on commercial air traffic, and sanctions on financial transactions. As conditions in Haiti worsened, President Clinton stated he would not rule out the use of force, and gradually the use of force appeared certain. Many Members continued to contend congressional authorization was necessary for any invasion of Haiti. On July 31, the U.N. Security Council authorized a multinational force to use "all necessary means to facilitate the departure from Haiti of the military leadership ... on the understanding that the cost of implementing this temporary operation will be borne by the participating Member States" (Resolution 940, 1994).

On August 3, the Senate adopted an amendment to the Department of Veterans Affairs appropriation, H.R. 4624, by a vote of 100-0 expressing its sense that the Security Council Resolution did not constitute authorization for the deployment of U.S. forces in Haiti under the Constitution or the War Powers Resolution, but the amendment was not agreed to in conference. President Clinton said the same day that he would welcome the support of Congress but did not agree that he was constitutionally mandated to obtain it. On September 15, 1994, in an address to the nation, President Clinton said he had called up the military reserve and ordered two aircraft carriers into the region. His message to the military dictators was to leave now or the United States would force them from power. The first phase of military action would remove the dictators from power and restore Haiti's democratically elected government. The second phase would involve a much smaller force joining with forces from other U.N. members which would leave Haiti after 1995 elections were held and a new government installed.

While the Defense Department continued to prepare for an invasion within days, on September 16 President Clinton sent to Haiti a negotiating team of former President Jimmy Carter, former Joint Chiefs of Staff Chairman Colin Powell, and Senate Armed Services Committee Chairman Sam Nunn. Again addressing the nation on September 18, President Clinton announced that the military leaders had agreed to step down by October 15, and agreed to the immediate introduction of troops from the 15,000-member international coalition beginning September 19. He said the agreement was only possible because of the credible and imminent threat of multinational force. He emphasized the mission still had risks and there remained possibilities of violence directed at U.S. troops, but the agreement minimized those risks. He also said that under U.N. Security Council resolution 940, a 25-nation international coalition would soon go to Haiti to begin the task of restoring democratic government. Also on September 18, President Clinton reported to Congress on the objectives in accordance with the sense expressed in Section 8147 (c) of P.L. 103-139, the FY1994 Defense Appropriations Act.

U.S. forces entered Haiti on September 19, 1994. On September 21, President Clinton reported "consistent with the War Powers Resolution" the deployment of 1,500 troops, to be increased by several thousand. (At the peak in September there were about 21,000 U.S. forces in Haiti.) He said the U.S. presence would not be open-ended but would be replaced after a period of months by a U.N. peacekeeping force, although some U.S. forces would participate in and be present for the duration of the U.N. mission. The forces were involved in the first hostilities on September 24, when U.S. Marines killed 10 armed Haitian resisters in a firefight.

On October 3, 1994, the House Foreign Affairs Committee reported H.J.Res. 416 authorizing the forces in Haiti until March 1, 1995, and providing procedures for a joint resolution to withdraw the forces. On October 6, the House adopted an amended text introduced by Representative Ron Dellums. As passed, H.J.Res. 416 stated the sense of the Congress that the President should have sought congressional approval before deploying U.S. forces to Haiti, supported a prompt and orderly withdrawal as soon as possible, and required a monthly report on Haiti as well as other reports. This same language was also adopted by the Senate on October 6 as S.J.Res. 229, and on October 7 the House passed S.J.Res. 229. President Clinton signed it on October 25, 1994 (P.L. 103-423).

After the U.S. forces began to disarm Haitian forces and President Aristide returned on October 15, 1994, the United States began to withdraw some forces. On March 31, 1995, U.N. peacekeeping forces assumed responsibility for missions previously conducted by U.S. military forces. By September 21, 1995, President Clinton reported the United States had 2,400 military personnel in Haiti as participants in the U.N. Mission in Haiti (UNMIH), and 260 U.S. military personnel assigned to the U.S. Support Group Haiti. On December 5, 1997, President Clinton stated that he intended to keep some military personnel in Haiti, even though United Nations peacekeeping forces were withdrawing. The Pentagon stated that U.S. military personnel in Haiti would be about 500, consisting mainly of engineering and medical units, with a combat element responsible for protecting the U.S. contingent. On March 2, 2004, the President reported to Congress "consistent with the War Powers Resolution" that, on February 29, he had sent about "200 additional U.S. combat-equipped, military personnel from the U.S. Joint Forces Command" to Port-au-Prince, Haiti, for a variety of purposes, including preparing the way for a U.N. Multinational Interim Force, and otherwise supporting U.N. Security Council Resolution 1529 (2004). For further information on Haiti, see CRS Report RL32294, *Haiti: Developments and U.S. Policy Since 1991 and Current Congressional Concerns*, by Maureen Taft-Morales and Clare Ribando Seelke.

Somalia

In Somalia, the participation of U.S. military forces in a U.N. operation to protect humanitarian assistance, which began in December 1992, became increasingly controversial as fighting and casualties increased and objectives appeared to be expanding. On October 7, 1993, President Clinton announced that all U.S. forces would be withdrawn by March 31, 1994, and most forces left by that date. The remaining 58 Marines, who had remained to protect U.S. diplomats, were withdrawn September 15, 1994.

A major issue for Congress was whether to authorize U.S. action in Somalia. On February 4, 1993, the Senate passed S.J.Res. 45 to authorize the President to use U.S. Armed Forces pursuant to U.N. Security Council Resolution 794. S.J.Res. 45 stated it was intended to constitute the specific statutory authorization under Section 5(b) of the War Powers Resolution. On May 25, 1993, the House amended and passed S.J.Res. 45. The amendment authorized U.S. forces to remain for one year. S.J.Res. 45 was then sent to the Senate for its concurrence, but the measure did not reach the floor.

As sporadic fighting resulted in the deaths of Somali and U.N. forces, including Americans, controversy over the operation intensified. On September 9, 1993, the Senate adopted an amendment to S. 1298, the Defense Authorization Bill, expressing the sense of Congress that the President by November 15, 1993, should seek and receive congressional authorization for the continued deployment of U.S. forces to Somalia. It asked that the President consult with Congress and report the goals, objectives, and anticipated jurisdiction of the U.S. mission in Somalia by October 15, 1993. On September 29, the House adopted a similar amendment to its bill, H.R. 2401. On October 7, the President consulted with congressional leaders from both parties for over two hours on Somalia policy and also announced that U.S. forces would be withdrawn by March 31, 1994.

On October 15, 1993, the Senate adopted an amendment by Senator Byrd to H.R. 3116, the Defense Department Appropriations Act for FY1994, cutting off funds for U.S. military operations in Somalia after March 31, 1994, unless the President obtained further spending authority from Congress. The Senate approved the use of military operations only for the protection of American military personnel and bases and for helping maintain the flow of relief aid by giving the U.N. forces security and logistical support. The amendment, which became Section 8151 of P.L. 103-139, required U.S. forces in Somalia to remain under the command and control of U.S. commanders. In addition, on November 9, 1993, the House adopted H.Con.Res.

170, using Section 5(c) of the War Powers Resolution to direct the President to remove forces from Somalia by March 31, 1994; sponsors stated it was a non-binding measure, and the Senate did not act on the measure. The Defense Appropriations Act for FY1995 (P.L. 103-335, signed September 30, 1994) prohibited the use of funds for the continuous presence of U.S. forces in Somalia, except for the protection of U.S. personnel, after September 30, 1994.

On November 4, the U.N. Security Council decided to end the U.N. mission in Somalia by March 31, 1995. On March 3, 1995, U.S. forces completed their assistance to United Nations forces evacuating Somalia.

Libya

On March 21, 2011, the President submitted to Congress, "consistent with the War Powers Resolution," a report stating that at "approximately 3:00 p.m. Eastern Daylight Time, on March 19, 2011," he had directed U.S. military forces to commence "operations to assist an international effort authorized by the United Nations (U.N.) Security Council and undertaken with the support of European allies and Arab partners, to prevent a humanitarian catastrophe and address the threat posed to international peace and security by the crisis in Libya." He further stated that U.S. military forces, "under the command of Commander, U.S. Africa Command, began a series of strikes against air defense systems and military airfields for the purposes of preparing a no-fly zone." These actions were part of "the multilateral response authorized under U.N. Security Council Resolution 1973," and the President added that "these strikes will be limited in their nature, duration, and scope. Their purpose is to support an international coalition as it takes all necessary measures to enforce the terms of U.N. Security Council Resolution 1973. These limited U.S. actions will set the stage for further action by other coalition partners."

The President noted that

> United Nations Security Council Resolution 1973 authorized Member States, under Chapter VII of the U.N. Charter, to take all necessary measures to protect civilians and civilian populated areas under threat of attack in Libya, including the establishment and enforcement of a "no-fly zone" in the airspace of Libya. United States military efforts are discrete and focused on employing unique U.S. military capabilities to set the conditions for our European allies and Arab partners to carry out the measures authorized by the U.N. Security Council Resolution.

The President stated further that the "United States has not deployed ground forces into Libya. United States forces are conducting a limited and well-defined mission in support of international efforts to protect civilians and prevent a humanitarian disaster." Accordingly, he added, "U.S. forces have targeted the Qadhafi regime's air defense systems, command and control structures, and other capabilities of Qadhafi's armed forces used to attack civilians and civilian populated areas." It was the intent of the United States, he said, to "seek a rapid, but responsible, transition of operations to coalition, regional, or international organizations that are postured to continue activities as may be necessary to realize the objectives of U.N. Security Council Resolutions 1970 and 1973."

The President said that the actions he had directed were "in the national security and foreign policy interests of the United States." He took them, the President stated, "pursuant to my constitutional authority to conduct U.S. foreign relations and as Commander in Chief and Chief Executive."

On April 1, 2011, the Office of Legal Counsel (OLC) of the U.S. Justice Department issued a memorandum opinion entitled "Authority to use Military Force in Libya" (made public on April 7, 2011), which detailed the advice provided to the Attorney General before President Obama commenced U.S. military operations in Libya. This opinion set out the legal reasoning behind the conclusions reached by OLC that the President's use of military force in Libya was constitutional because he "could reasonably determine that such use of force was in the national interest." It was also the opinion of OLC that "prior congressional approval was not constitutionally required to use military force in the limited operations under consideration." The full text of this opinion is found in the opinions section of the OLC webpage: http://www.justice.gov/olc/memoranda-opinions.html.

The Office of Legal Counsel opinion of April 1, 2011, on Military Force in Libya cites a number of previous opinions of OLC, and various Supreme Court cases, as providing the framework for its analysis and conclusions. Among these previous OLC opinions cited that address presidential authority to use U.S. Armed Forces overseas are the following: "Authorization for Continuing Hostilities in Kosovo," December 19, 2000, in 24 Op. OLC (2000); "Proposed Bosnia Deployment," November 30, 1995, in 19 Op. OLC (1995); "Deployment of United States Armed Forces into Haiti," September 27, 1994, in 18 Op. OLC (1994); "Authority to use United States Military Forces in Somalia," December 4, 1992, in 16 Op. OLC (1992); and "Presidential Power to Use the Armed Forces Abroad Without Statutory Authorization" February 12, 1980, in 4A Op. OLC (1980).

Having reviewed its prior opinions and Supreme Court holdings on cases deemed germane, the Office of Legal Counsel stated that determining the

> President's legal authority to direct military force in Libya turns on two questions: first, whether United States operations in Libya would serve sufficiently important national interests to permit the President's action as Commander in Chief and Chief Executive and pursuant to his authority to conduct U.S. foreign relations; and second, whether the military operations that the President anticipated ordering would be sufficiently extensive in "nature, scope, and duration" to constitute a "war" requiring prior specific congressional approval under the Declaration of War Clause.

Given this predicate, the OLC concluded that: "In our view, the combination of at least two national interests that the President reasonably determined were at stake here—preserving regional stability and supporting the UNSC's [United Nations Security Council] credibility and effectiveness—provided a sufficient basis for the President's exercise of his constitutional authority to order the use of military force." The OLC also concluded that "we do not believe that anticipated United States operations in Libya amounted to a 'war' in the constitutional sense necessitating congressional approval under the Declaration of War Clause." Thus, the Office of Legal Counsel stated, "Accordingly, we conclude that President Obama could rely on his constitutional power to safeguard the national interest by directing the anticipated military operations in Libya—which were limited in their nature, scope, and duration—without prior congressional authorization."

On May 20, 2011, President Obama sent a letter to the leaders of the Congress, on the 60th day since he had initiated the use of U.S. military personnel to support a "no-fly zone" over Libya, and to "prevent a humanitarian catastrophe" by protecting "the people of Libya from the Qaddafi regime." He noted that since April 4 the United States had "transferred responsibility for the military operations in Libya to the North Atlantic Treaty Organization (NATO) and the U.S. involvement has assumed a supporting role in the coalition's efforts." The President further stated that since April 4, U.S. participation in this endeavor had "consisted of: (1) non-kinetic support to the NATO –led operation, including intelligence, logistical support, and search and rescue assistance; (2) aircraft that have assisted in the suppression and destruction of air defenses in support of the no-fly zone; and (3) since April 23, precision strikes by unmanned aerial vehicles against a limited set of clearly defined targets in support of the NATO-led coalition's efforts." President Obama stated that despite the fact that the United States was "no longer in the lead" of the operation in Libya, "U.S. support for the NATO-based coalition" remained "crucial to assuring the success of the international efforts to protect civilians from the actions of the Qaddafi regime." He further stated that "Congressional action in support of the mission would underline the U.S. commitment to this remarkable international effort." In this regard, the President expressly stated his "support for the bipartisan resolution drafted by Senators Kerry, McCain, Levin, Feinstein, Graham, and Lieberman," which he believed would "confirm that the Congress supports the U.S. mission in Libya and that both branches are united in their commitment to supporting the aspirations of the Libyan people for political reform and self-government." It would also, he concluded, "demonstrate a unity of purpose among the political branches on this important national security matter."

On June 3, 2011, the House defeated, by a vote of 148 yeas to 265 nays, H.Con.Res. 51, which said that "pursuant to section 5(c) of the War Powers Resolution … Congress directs the President to remove the United States Armed Forces from Libya by not later than the date that is 15 days after the date of the adoption of this concurrent resolution."

On June 3, 2011, the House passed, by a vote of 268 yeas to 145 nays, H.Res. 292, expressing the opinion of the House, among other things, that "the President shall not deploy, establish or maintain the presence of units and members of the United States Armed Forces on the ground in Libya," except to rescue a member of the Armed Forces from imminent danger, and that the President shall within 14 days after passage of this resolution provide a report to the House detailing information about Operation Odyssey Dawn and Operation Unified Protector, and a report answering a number of questions detailing U.S. security interests and objectives, and the activities of United States Armed Forces, in Libya since March 19, 2011. H.Res. 292 also made the following findings: (1) that the President "has not sought, and Congress has not provided, authorization for the introduction or continued involvement of the United States Armed Forces in Libya," and (2) that "Congress has the constitutional prerogative to withhold funding for any unauthorized use of the United States Armed Forces, including for unauthorized activities regarding Libya."

On June 15, 2011, the Obama Administration submitted a 32-page unclassified report, together with a classified annex, that described U.S. actions in Libya to that date. On page 25 of that report was a "Legal Analysis" consisting of one long paragraph summarizing the Administration's view of what the President's authority was to take the actions he had taken in Libya, and his rationale for not having to obtain congressional authorization to do so. This paragraph from the report states:

> Given the important U.S. interests served by U.S. military operations in Libya and the limited nature, scope and duration of the anticipated actions, the President had constitutional authority, as Commander in Chief and Chief Executive and pursuant to his foreign affairs powers, to direct such limited military operations abroad. The President is of the view that the current U.S. military operations in Libya are consistent with the War Powers Resolution and do not under that law require further congressional authorization, because U.S. military operations are distinct from the kind of "hostilities" contemplated by the Resolution's 60 day termination provision. U.S. forces are playing a constrained and supporting role in a

multinational coalition, whose operations are both legitimated by and limited to the terms of a United Nations Security Council Resolution that authorizes the use of force solely to protect civilians and civilian populated areas under attack or threat of attack and to enforce a no-fly zone and an arms embargo. U.S. operations do not involve sustained fighting or active exchanges of fire with hostile forces, nor do they involve the presence of U.S. ground troops, U.S. casualties or a serious threat thereof, or any significant chance of escalation into a conflict characterized by these factors.

Regarding the prospect of receiving congressional support for the President's action in Libya, the report of June 15, 2011, also stated on page 25 that:

> The Administration has repeatedly indicated its strong support for the bipartisan resolution drafted by Senators McCain, Kerry, Lieberman, Levin, Feinstein, Graham, and Chambliss that would confirm that both branches are united in their commitment to supporting the aspirations of the Libyan people for political reform and self-government.

On June 24, 2011, the House of Representatives, by a vote of 123 yeas to 295 nays, defeated H.J.Res. 68, which would have authorized the limited use of the United States Armed Forces in support of the NATO mission in Libya. Subsequently, on June 24, 2011, the House of Representatives, by a vote of 180 yeas to 238 nays, defeated H.R. 2278, which would have limited the use of funds appropriated to the Department of Defense for United States Armed Forces in support of North Atlantic Treaty Organization Operation Unified Protector with respect to Libya, unless otherwise specifically authorized by law.

Instances Formally Reported Under the War Powers Resolution

Presidents have submitted 132 reports to Congress as a result of the War Powers Resolution. Of these, President Ford submitted 4, President Carter 1, President Reagan 14, President George H. W. Bush 7, President Clinton 60, President George W. Bush 39, and President Barack Obama 11. For a summary of the 111 reports submitted by the Presidents from 1975-2009, see CRS Report R41199, *The War Powers Resolution: After Thirty-Six Years*, by Richard F. Grimmett. The following is a brief summary of reports submitted by President Bush George W. Bush from January 2004-December 2008, and by President Barack Obama since January 2009. The reports are submitted to the Speaker of the House in a formal communication (the President pro tempore of the Senate also receives a copy of each report), and they are subsequently published on the U.S. government printing office website under House Documents. The full texts of these presidential reports may be found at http://www.gpoaccess.gov/serialset/cdocuments/index.html. More recent copies of these presidential reports may be found in the Daily Compilation of Presidential Documents at http://www.gpo.gov/fdsys/browse/collection.action?collectionCode= CDOC. They are also found in Public Papers section of the American Presidency Project at http://www.presidency.ucsb.edu/ws/#axzz1dzdN7PmM.

(112) On January 22, 2004, the President reported to Congress "consistent with the War Powers Resolution" that the United States was continuing to deploy combat equipped military personnel in Bosnia and Herzegovina in support of NATO's Stabilization Force (SFOR) and its peacekeeping efforts in this country. About 1,800 U.S. personnel are participating.

(113) On February 25, 2004, the President reported to Congress "consistent with the War Powers Resolution" that, on February 23, he had sent a combat-equipped "security force" of about "55 U.S. military personnel from the U.S. Joint Forces Command" to Port-au-Prince, Haiti, to augment the U.S. Embassy security forces there and to protect American citizens and property in light of the instability created by the armed rebellion in Haiti.

(114) On March 2, 2004, the President reported to Congress "consistent with the War Powers Resolution" that on February 29 he had sent about "200 additional U.S. combat-equipped, military personnel from the U.S. Joint Forces Command" to Port-au-Prince, Haiti, for a variety of purposes, including preparing the way for a U.N. Multinational Interim Force, and otherwise supporting U.N. Security Council Resolution 1529 (2004).

(115) On March 20, 2004, the President sent to Congress "consistent with the War Powers Resolution," a consolidated report giving details of multiple ongoing United States military deployments and operations "in support of the global war on terrorism (including in Afghanistan)," as well as operations in Bosnia and Herzegovina, Kosovo, and Haiti. In this report, the President noted that U.S. anti-terror related activities were underway in Georgia, Djibouti, Kenya, Ethiopia, Yemen, and Eritrea. He further noted that U.S. combat-equipped military personnel continued to be deployed in Kosovo as part of the NATO-led KFOR (1,900 personnel); in Bosnia and Herzegovina as part of the NATO-led SFOR (about 1,100 personnel); and approximately 1,800 military personnel were deployed in Haiti as part of the U.N. Multinational Interim Force.

(116) On November 4, 2004, the President sent to Congress, "consistent with the War Powers Resolution," a consolidated report giving details of multiple ongoing United States military deployments and operations "in support of the global war on terrorism." These deployments, support or military operations include activities in Afghanistan, Djibouti, as well as Kenya, Ethiopia, Eritrea, Bosnia and Herzegovina, and Kosovo. In this report, the President noted that U.S. anti-terror related activities were underway in Djibouti, Kenya, Ethiopia, Yemen, and Eritrea. He further noted that U.S. combat-equipped military personnel continued to be deployed in Kosovo as part of the NATO-led KFOR (1,800 personnel); and in Bosnia and Herzegovina as part of the NATO-led SFOR (about 1,000 personnel). Meanwhile, he stated that the United States continues to deploy more than 135,000 military personnel in Iraq.

(117) On May 20, 2005, the President sent to Congress "consistent with the War Powers Resolution," a consolidated report giving details of multiple ongoing United States military deployments and operations "in support of the global war on terrorism," as well as operations in Iraq, where currently about 139,000 U.S. military personnel are stationed. U.S. forces are also deployed in Kenya, Ethiopia, Yemen, Eritrea, and Djibouti assisting in "enhancing counter-terrorism capabilities" of these nations. The President further noted that U.S. combat-equipped military personnel continued to be deployed in Kosovo as part of the NATO-led KFOR (1,700 personnel). Approximately 235 U.S. personnel are also deployed in Bosnia and Herzegovina as part of the NATO Headquarters-Sarajevo who assist in defense reform and perform operational tasks, such as counter-terrorism and supporting the International Criminal Court for the Former Yugoslavia.

(118) On December 7, 2005, the President sent to Congress "consistent" with the War Powers Resolution, a consolidated report giving details of multiple ongoing United States military deployments and operations "in support of the global war on terrorism," and in support of the Multinational Force in Iraq, where about 160,000 U.S. military personnel are deployed. U.S.

forces are also deployed in the Horn of Africa region—Kenya, Ethiopia, Yemen, and Djibouti—assisting in "enhancing counter-terrorism capabilities" of these nations. The President further noted that U.S. combat-equipped military personnel continued to be deployed in Kosovo as part of the NATO-led KFOR (1,700 personnel). Approximately 220 U.S. personnel are also deployed in Bosnia and Herzegovina as part of the NATO Headquarters-Sarajevo who assist in defense reform and perform operational tasks, such as "counter-terrorism and supporting the International Criminal Court for the Former Yugoslavia."

(119) On June 15, 2006, the President sent to Congress "consistent" with the War Powers Resolution, a consolidated report giving details of multiple ongoing United States military deployments and operations "in support of the war on terror," and in Kosovo, Bosnia and Herzegovina, and as part of the Multinational Force (MNF) in Iraq. Presently, about 131,000 military personnel were deployed in Iraq. U.S. forces were also deployed in the Horn of Africa region, and in Djibouti to support necessary operations against al-Qaida and other international terrorists operating in the region. U.S. military personnel continue to support the NATO-led Kosovo Force (KFOR). The current U.S. contribution to KFOR is about 1,700 military personnel. The NATO Headquarters-Sarajevo was established in November 22, 2004, as a successor to its stabilization operations in Bosnia-Herzegovina to continue to assist in implementing the peace agreement. Approximately 250 U.S. personnel are assigned to the NATO Headquarters-Sarajevo who assist in defense reform and perform operational tasks, such as "counter-terrorism and supporting the International Criminal Court for the Former Yugoslavia."

(120) On July 18, 2006, the President reported to Congress "consistent" with the War Powers Resolution, that in response to the security threat posed in Lebanon to "U.S. Embassy personnel and citizens and designated third country personnel," he had deployed combat-equipped military helicopters and military personnel to Beirut to assist in the departure of the persons under threat from Lebanon. The President noted that additional combat-equipped U.S. military forces may be deployed "to Lebanon, Cyprus and other locations, as necessary." to assist further departures of persons from Lebanon and to provide security. He further stated that once the threat to U.S. citizens and property has ended, the U.S. military forces would redeploy.

(121) On December 15, 2006, the President sent to Congress "consistent" with the War Powers Resolution, a consolidated report giving details of multiple ongoing United States military deployments and operations "in support of the war on terror," in Kosovo, Bosnia and Herzegovina, and as part of the Multinational Force (MNF) in Iraq. Presently, about 134,000 military personnel are deployed in Iraq. U.S. forces were also deployed in the Horn of Africa region, and in Djibouti to support necessary operations against al-Qaida and other international terrorists operating in the region, including Yemen. U.S. military personnel continue to support the NATO-led Kosovo Force (KFOR). The current U.S. contribution to KFOR is about 1,700 military personnel. The NATO Headquarters-Sarajevo was established in November 22, 2004, as a successor to its stabilization operations in Bosnia-Herzegovina to continue to assist in implementing the peace agreement. Approximately 100 U.S. personnel are assigned to the NATO Headquarters-Sarajevo to assist in defense reform and perform operational tasks, such as "counter-terrorism and supporting the International Criminal Court for the Former Yugoslavia."

(122) On June 15, 2007, the President sent to Congress "consistent" with the War Powers Resolution, a consolidated report giving details of ongoing United States military deployments and operations "in support of the war on terror," and in support of the NATO-led Kosovo Force (KFOR). The President reported that various U.S. "combat-equipped and combat-support forces" were deployed to "a number of locations in the Central, Pacific, European (KFOR), and Southern

Command areas of operation" and were engaged in combat operations against al-Qaida terrorists and their supporters. The United States is currently "pursuing and engaging remnant al-Qaida and Taliban fighters in Afghanistan." U.S. forces in Afghanistan currently total approximately 25,945. Of this total, "approximately 14,340 are assigned to the International Security Assistance Force (ISAF) in Afghanistan." The U.S. military continues to support peacekeeping operations in Kosovo, specifically the NATO-led Kosovo Force (KFOR). Currently, the U.S. contribution to KFOR in Kosovo is approximately 1,584 military personnel.

(123) On December 14, 2007, the President sent to Congress "consistent with the War Powers Resolution," a consolidated report giving details of ongoing United States military deployments and operations "in support of the war on terror," and in support of the NATO-led Kosovo Force (KFOR). The President reported that various U.S. "combat-equipped and combat-support forces" were deployed to "a number of locations in the Central, Pacific, European, and Southern Command areas of operation" and were engaged in combat operations against al-Qaida terrorists and their supporters. The United States is currently "pursuing and engaging remnant al-Qaida and Taliban fighters in Afghanistan." U.S. forces in Afghanistan currently total approximately 25,900. Of this total, "approximately 15,180 are assigned to the International Security Assistance Force (ISAF) in Afghanistan." The U.S. military continues to support peacekeeping operations in Kosovo, specifically the NATO-led Kosovo Force (KFOR). Currently, the U.S. contribution to KFOR in Kosovo is approximately 1,498 military personnel.

(124) On June 13, 2008, the President sent to Congress "consistent with the War Powers Resolution," a consolidated report giving details of ongoing United States military deployments and operations "in support of the war on terror," and in support of the NATO-led Kosovo Force (KFOR). The President reported that various U.S. "combat-equipped and combat-support forces" were deployed to "a number of locations in the Central, Pacific, European, and Southern Command areas of operation" and were engaged in combat operations against al-Qaida terrorists and their supporters. The United States is currently "pursuing and engaging remnant al-Qaida and Taliban fighters in Afghanistan." U.S. forces in Afghanistan currently total approximately 31,122. Of this total, "approximately 14,275 are assigned to the International Security Assistance Force (ISAF) in Afghanistan." The U.S. military continues to support peacekeeping operations in Kosovo, specifically the NATO-led Kosovo Force (KFOR). Currently, the U.S. contribution to KFOR in Kosovo is about 1,500 military personnel.

(125) On December 16, 2008, the President sent to Congress "consistent with the War Powers Resolution," a consolidated report giving details of ongoing United States military deployments and operations "in support of the war on terror," and in support of the NATO-led Kosovo Force (KFOR). The President reported that various U.S. "combat-equipped and combat-support forces" were deployed to "a number of locations in the Central, Pacific, European, Southern, and Africa Command areas of operation" and were engaged in combat operations against al-Qaida and their supporters. The United States is "actively pursuing and engaging remnant al-Qaida and Taliban fighters in Afghanistan." U.S. forces in Afghanistan total approximately 31,000. Of this total, "approximately 13,000 are assigned to the International Security Assistance Force (ISAF) in Afghanistan." The U.S. military continues to support peacekeeping operations in Kosovo, specifically the NATO-led Kosovo Force (KFOR). The current U.S. contribution to KFOR in Kosovo is about 1,500 military personnel.

(126) On June 15, 2009, the President sent to Congress "consistent with the War Powers Resolution," a supplemental consolidated report, giving details of "ongoing contingency operations overseas." The report noted that the total number of U.S. forces in Afghanistan was

"approximately 58,000," of which approximately 20,000 are assigned to the International Security Assistance Force (ISAF) in Afghanistan." The United States continues to pursue and engage "remaining al-Qa'ida and Taliban forces in Afghanistan." The U.S. also continues to deploy military forces in support of the Multinational Force (MNF) in Iraq. The current U.S. contribution to this effort is "approximately 138,000 U.S. military personnel." U.S. military operations continue in Kosovo, as part of the NATO-led Kosovo Force (KFOR). Presently the United States contributes approximately 1,400 U.S. military personnel to KFOR. In addition, the United States continues to deploy "U.S. combat-equipped forces to help enhance the counterterrorism capabilities of our friends and allies" not only in the Horn of Africa region, but globally through "maritime interception operations on the high seas" aimed at blocking the "movement, arming and financing of international terrorists."

(127) On December 16, 2009, the President sent to Congress "consistent with the War Powers Resolution," a consolidated report, giving details of "global deployments of U.S. Armed Forces equipped for combat." The report detailed "ongoing U.S. contingency operations overseas." The report noted that the total number of U.S. forces in Afghanistan was "approximately 68,000," of which approximately 34,000 are assigned to the International Security Assistance Force (ISAF) in Afghanistan. The United States continues to pursue and engage "remaining al-Qa'ida and Taliban forces in Afghanistan." The United States has deployed "various combat-equipped forces to a number of locations in the Central, Pacific, European, Southern and African Command areas of operation" in support of anti-terrorist and anti-al-Qa'ida actions. The United States also continues to deploy military forces in Iraq to "maintain security and stability" there. These Iraqi operations continue pursuant to the terms of a bilateral agreement between the United States and Iraq, which entered into force on January 1, 2009. The current U.S. force level in Iraq is "approximately 116,000 U.S. military personnel." U.S. military operations continue in Kosovo, as part of the NATO-led Kosovo Force (KFOR). Presently the United States contributes approximately 1,475 U.S. military personnel to KFOR. In addition, the United States continues to deploy "U.S. combat-equipped forces to assist in enhancing the counterterrorism capabilities of our friends and allies" not only in the Horn of Africa region, but globally through "maritime interception operations on the high seas" aimed at blocking the "movement, arming and financing of international terrorists."

(128) On June 15, 2010, the President sent to Congress "consistent with the War Powers Resolution," a consolidated report, giving details of "deployments of U.S. Armed Forces equipped for combat." The report noted that the total number of U.S. forces in Afghanistan was "approximately 87,000," of which over 62,000 are assigned to the International Security Assistance Force (ISAF) in Afghanistan. The United States continues combat operations "against al-Qa'ida terrorists and their Taliban supporters" in Afghanistan. The United States has deployed "combat-equipped forces to a number of locations in the U.S. Central, Pacific, European, Southern and African Command areas of operation" in support of anti-terrorist and anti-al-Qa'ida actions. The United States also continues to deploy military forces in Iraq to "maintain security and stability" there. These Iraqi operations continue pursuant to the terms of a bilateral agreement between the United States and Iraq, which entered into force on January 1, 2009. The current U.S. force level in Iraq is "approximately 95,000 U.S. military personnel." U.S. military operations continue in Kosovo, as part of the NATO-led Kosovo Force (KFOR). Presently, the United States contributes approximately 1,074 U.S. military personnel to KFOR. In addition, the United States continues to "conduct maritime interception operations on the high seas" directed at "stopping the movement, arming and financing of international terrorist groups."

(129) On December 15, 2010, the President submitted to Congress "consistent with the War Powers Resolution," a consolidated report, detailing "deployments of U.S. Armed Forces equipped for combat." The report noted that the total number of U.S. forces in Afghanistan was "approximately 97,500," of which over 81,500 were assigned to the International Security Assistance Force (ISAF) in Afghanistan. The United States is continuing combat operations "against al-Qa'ida terrorists and their Taliban supporters" in Afghanistan. The United States has deployed "combat-equipped forces to a number of locations in the U.S. Central, Pacific, European, Southern and African Command areas of operation" in support of anti-terrorist and anti-al-Qa'ida actions. In addition, the United States continues to conduct "maritime interception operations on the high seas in the areas of responsibility of the geographic combatant commands" directed at "stopping the movement, arming and financing of international terrorist groups." The United States also continues to deploy military forces in Iraq in support of Iraqi efforts to "maintain security and stability" there. These Iraqi operations continue pursuant to the terms of a bilateral agreement between the United States and Iraq, which entered into force on January 1, 2009. The current U.S. force level in Iraq is "approximately 48,400 U.S. military personnel." U.S. military operations also continue in Kosovo, as part of the NATO-led Kosovo Force (KFOR). The United States currently contributes approximately 808 U.S. military personnel to KFOR.

(130) On June 15, 2011, the President sent to Congress, "consistent with the War Powers Resolution," a supplemental consolidated report, giving details of "global deployments of U.S. Armed Forces equipped for combat." The report detailed ongoing U.S. contingency operations overseas. The report noted that the total number of U.S. forces in Afghanistan was "approximately 99,000," of which approximately 83,000 are assigned to the International Security Assistance Force (ISAF) in Afghanistan. The United States continues to pursue and engage "remaining al-Qa'ida and Taliban fighters in Afghanistan." The United States has deployed various "combat-equipped forces" to a number of locations in the Central, Pacific, European, Southern and African Command areas of operation" in support of anti-terrorist and anti-al-Qa'ida actions. This includes the deployment of U.S. military forces globally to assist in enhancing the counterterrorism capabilities of our friends and allies through maritime interception operations on the high seas "aimed at stopping the movement, arming and financing of certain international terrorist groups." A combat-equipped security force of about "40 U.S. military personnel from the U.S. Central Command" was deployed to Cairo, Egypt, on January 31, 2011, for the sole purpose of "protecting American citizens and property." That force remains at the U.S. Embassy in Cairo. The United States also continues to deploy military forces in Iraq to help it "maintain security and stability" there. These Iraqi operations continue pursuant to the terms of a bilateral agreement between the United States and Iraq, which entered into force on January 1, 2009. The current U.S. force level in Iraq is approximately 45,000 U.S. military personnel. In Libya, since April 4, 2011, the United States has transferred responsibility for military operations there to NATO, and U.S. involvement "has assumed a supporting role in the coalition's efforts." U.S. support in Libya has been limited to "intelligence, logistical support, and search and rescue assistance." The U.S. military aircraft have also been used to assist in the "suppression and destruction of air defenses in support of the no-fly zone" over Libya. Since April 23, 2011, the United States has supported the coalition effort in Libya through use of "unmanned aerial vehicles against a limited set of clearly defined targets" there. Except in the case of operations to "rescue the crew of a U.S. aircraft" on March 21, 2011, "the United States has deployed no ground forces to Libya." U.S. military operations continue in Kosovo, as part of the NATO-led Kosovo Force (KFOR). Presently the United States contributes approximately 800 U.S. military personnel to KFOR.

(131) On March 21, 2011, the President submitted to Congress "consistent with the War Powers Resolution," a report stating that at "approximately 3:00 p.m. Eastern Daylight Time, on March 19, 2011," he had directed U.S. military forces to commence "operations to assist an international effort authorized by the United Nations (U.N.) Security Council and undertaken with the support of European allies and Arab partners, to prevent a humanitarian catastrophe and address the threat posed to international peace and security by the crisis in Libya." He further stated that U.S. military forces, "under the command of Commander, U.S. Africa Command, began a series of strikes against air defense systems and military airfields for the purposes of preparing a no-fly zone." These actions were part of "the multilateral response authorized under U.N. Security Council Resolution 1973," and the President added that "these strikes will be limited in their nature, duration, and scope. Their purpose is to support an international coalition as it takes all necessary measures to enforce the terms of U.N. Security Council Resolution 1973. These limited U.S. actions will set the stage for further action by other coalition partners."

The President noted that

> United Nations Security Council Resolution 1973 authorized Member States, under Chapter VII of the U.N. Charter, to take all necessary measures to protect civilians and civilian populated areas under threat of attack in Libya, including the establishment and enforcement of a "no-fly zone" in the airspace of Libya. United States military efforts are discrete and focused on employing unique U.S. military capabilities to set the conditions for our European allies and Arab partners to carry out the measures authorized by the U.N. Security Council Resolution.

The President stated further that the "United States has not deployed ground forces into Libya. United States forces are conducting a limited and well-defined mission in support of international efforts to protect civilians and prevent a humanitarian disaster." Accordingly, he added, "U.S. forces have targeted the Qadhafi regime's air defense systems, command and control structures, and other capabilities of Qadhafi's armed forces used to attack civilians and civilian populated areas." It was the intent of the United States, he said, to "seek a rapid, but responsible, transition of operations to coalition, regional, or international organizations that are postured to continue activities as may be necessary to realize the objectives of U.N. Security Council Resolutions 1970 and 1973."

The President said that the actions he had directed were "in the national security and foreign policy interests of the United States." He took them, the President stated, "pursuant to my constitutional authority to conduct U.S. foreign relations and as Commander in Chief and Chief Executive."

(132) On October 14, 2011, the President submitted to Congress, "consistent with the War Powers Resolution," a report stating that "he had authorized a small number of combat-equipped U.S. forces to deploy to central Africa to provide assistance to regional forces that are working toward the removal of Joseph Kony," leader of the Lord's Resistance Army (LRA), from the battlefield. For over two decades the LRA has murdered, kidnapped, and raped tens of thousands of men, women, and children throughout central Africa, and has continued to commit atrocities in South Sudan, the Democratic Republic of the Congo, and the Central African Republic. The U.S. Armed Forces, the President noted, would be a "significant contribution toward counter-LRA efforts in central Africa." The President stated that on "October 12, 2011, the initial team of U.S. military personnel with appropriate combat equipment deployed to Uganda." In the "next month, additional forces will deploy, including a second combat-equipped team and associated headquarters, communications, and logistics personnel." The President further stated that the

"total number of U.S. military personnel deploying for this mission is approximately 100. These forces will act as advisors to partner forces that have the goals of removing from the battlefield Joseph Kony and other senior leadership of the LRA." U.S. forces "will provide information, advice, and assistance to select partner nation forces." With the approval of the respective host nations, "elements of these U.S. forces will deploy into Uganda, South Sudan, the Central African Republic, and the Democratic Republic of the Congo. The support provided by U.S. forces will enhance regional efforts against the LRA." The President emphasized that even though the "U.S. forces are combat-equipped, they will only be providing information, advice, and assistance to partner nation forces, and they will not themselves engage LRA forces unless necessary for self-defense. All appropriate precautions have been taken to ensure the safety of U.S. military personnel during their deployment." The President took note in his report that Congress had previously "expressed support for increased, comprehensive U.S. efforts to help mitigate and eliminate the threat posed by the LRA to civilians and regional stability" through the passage of the Lord's Resistance Army Disarmament and Northern Uganda Recovery Act of 2009, P.L. 111-172, enacted May 24, 2010.

(133) On December 15, 2011, the President submitted to Congress, "consistent with the War Powers Resolution," a supplemental consolidated report, giving details of "deployments of U.S. Armed Forces equipped for combat." The report detailed ongoing U.S. contingency operations overseas. The report noted that the total number of U.S. forces in Afghanistan was "approximately 93,000," of which approximately 78,000 are assigned to the International Security Assistance Force (ISAF) in Afghanistan. The United States continues to pursue and engage "remaining al-Qa'ida and Taliban fighters in Afghanistan." The United States has deployed various "combat-equipped forces" to a number of locations in the Central, Pacific, European, Southern and African Command areas of operation in support of anti-terrorist and anti-al-Qa'ida actions. This includes the deployment of U.S. military forces globally: "including special operations and other forces" for "sensitive operations" in various places, as well as forces to assist in enhancing the counterterrorism capabilities of our friends and allies. U.S. forces also have engaged in maritime interception operations on the high seas "aimed at stopping the movement, arming and financing of certain international terrorist groups." The United States continued to deploy military forces in Iraq to help it "maintain security and stability" there. These Iraqi operations were undertaken pursuant to the terms of a bilateral agreement between the United States and Iraq, which entered into force on January 1, 2009. The U.S. force level in Iraq on October 28, 2011, was "36,001 U.S. military personnel." The United States was committed to withdraw U.S. forces from Iraq by December 31, 2011. [This occurred, as scheduled, after this report was submitted]. In Libya, after April 4, 2011, the United States transferred responsibility for military operations there to NATO, and U.S. involvement "assumed a supporting role in the coalition's efforts." U.S. support in Libya was limited to "intelligence, logistical support, and search and rescue assistance." The U.S. military aircraft were also used to assist in the "suppression and destruction of air defenses in support of the no-fly zone" over Libya. After April 23, 2011, the United States supported the coalition effort in Libya through use of "unmanned aerial vehicles against a limited set of clearly defined targets" there. Except in the case of operations to "rescue the crew of a U.S. aircraft" on March 21, 2011, and deploying 16 U.S. military personnel to aid in re-establishing the U.S. Embassy in Tripoli in September 2011, "the U.S. deployed no ground forces to Libya." On October 27, 2011, the United Nations terminated the "no-fly zone" effective October 31, 2011. NATO terminated its mission during this same time. U.S. military operations continue in Kosovo, as part of the NATO-led Kosovo Force (KFOR). Presently the United States contributes approximately 800 U.S. military personnel to KFOR.

(134) On January 26, 2012, the President submitted to Congress, "consistent with the War Powers Resolution," a report detailing a successful U.S. Special Operations Forces operation in Somalia of January 24, 2012 to rescue Ms. Jessica Buchanan, a U.S. citizen who had been kidnapped by a group linked to Somali pirates and financiers. This operation was undertaken "by a small number of joint combat-equipped U.S. forces" following receipt of reliable intelligence establishing her location in Somalia. A Danish national Poul Hagen Thisted, kidnapped with Ms. Buchanan, was also rescued with her.

(135) On June 15, 2012, the President reported to Congress, "consistent with" the War Powers Resolution, a consolidated report regarding various deployments of U.S. Armed Forces equipped for combat. In the efforts in support of U.S. counterterrorism (CT) objectives against al-Qa'ida, the Taliban, and associated forces, he noted that U.S. forces were engaged in Afghanistan in the above effort were "approximately 90,000." With regard to other counter-terrorism operations, the President stated that the United States had deployed "U.S. combat-equipped forces to assist in enhancing the CT capabilities of our friends and allies including special operations and other forces for sensitive operations in various locations around the world. He noted that the "U.S. military has taken direct action in Somalia against members of al-Qa'ida, including those who are also members of al-Shabaab, who are engaged in efforts to carry out terrorist attacks against the United States and our interests." The President further stated that the U.S. military had been "working closely with the Yemini government to operationally and ultimately eliminate the terrorist threat posed by al-Qa-ida in the Arabian Peninsula (AQAP), the most active and dangerous affiliate of al-Qa'ida today." He added that these "joint efforts have resulted in direct action against a limited number of AQAP operatives and senior leaders in that country who posed a terrorist threat to the United States and our interests." The President noted that he would direct "additional measures against al-Qa'ida, the Taliban, and associated forces to protect U.S. citizens and interests." Further information on such matters is provided in a "classified annex to this report."

Other military operations reported by the President include the deployment of U.S. combat-equipped military personnel to Uganda "to serve as advisors to regional forces that are working to apprehend or remove Joseph Kony and other senior Lord's Resistance Army (LRA) leaders from the battlefield and to protect local populations." The total number of U.S. military personnel deployed for this mission is "approximately 90," and elements of these U.S. forces have been sent to "forward locations in the LRA-affected areas of the Republic of South Sudan, the Democratic Republic of the Congo, and the Central African Republic." These U.S. forces "will not engage LRA forces except in self-defense."

The President also reported that presently the United States was contributing "approximately 817 military personnel: to the NATO-led Kosovo Force (KFOR) in Kosovo." He also reported that the United States remained prepared to engage in "maritime interception operations" intended to stop the "movement, arming, and financing of certain international terrorist groups," as well as stopping "proliferation by sea of weapons of mass destruction and related materials." Additional details about these efforts are included in "the classified annex" to the President's report.

(136) On September 14, 2012, the President reported to Congress, "consistent with" the War Powers Resolution, that on September 12, 2012, he ordered deployed to Libya "a security force from the U.S. Africa Command" to "support the security of U.S. personnel in Libya." This action was taken in response to the attack on the U.S. "diplomatic post in Benghazi, Libya" that had killed four America citizens, including U.S. Ambassador John Christopher Stevens. The President added on September 13, 2012, that "an additional security force arrived in Yemen in response to

security threats there." He further stated that: "Although these security forces are equipped for combat, these movements have been undertaken solely for the purpose of protecting American citizens and property." These security forces will remain in Libya and in Yemen, he noted, "until the security situation becomes such that they are no longer needed."

Consultation with Congress

Section 3 of the War Powers Resolution requires the President "in every possible instance" to consult with Congress before introducing U.S. Armed Forces into situations of hostilities and imminent hostilities, and to continue consultations as long as the Armed Forces remain. A review of instances involving the use of Armed Forces since passage of the Resolution, noted in this report, indicates there has been very little consultation with Congress under the Resolution when consultation is defined to mean seeking advice prior to a decision to introduce troops. Presidents have met with congressional leaders after the decision to deploy was made but before commencement of operations.

One problem is the interpretation of when consultation is required. The War Powers Resolution established different criteria for consultation than for reporting. Consultation is required only before introducing Armed Forces into "hostilities or into situations where imminent involvement in hostilities is clearly indicated by the circumstances," the circumstances triggering the time limit. A second problem is the meaning of the term consultation. The executive branch has often taken the view that the consultation requirement has been fulfilled when from the viewpoint of some Members of Congress it has not. The House report on the War Powers Resolution said, "consultation in this provision means that a decision is pending on a problem and that Members of Congress are being asked by the President for their advice and opinions and, in appropriate circumstances, their approval of action contemplated." A third problem is who represents Congress for consultation purposes. The House version specifically called for consultation between the President and the leadership and appropriate committees. This was changed to less specific wording in final House-Senate conference committee version, to provide some flexibility. Some critics of the existing statute have introduced proposals to specify a consultation group. But Congress has yet to act on such a proposal.

Issues for Congress

An immediate issue for Congress when the President introduces troops into situations of potential hostilities is whether to invoke Section 4(a)(1) of the War Powers Resolution and trigger a durational limit for the action unless Congress authorizes the forces to remain. If Congress concurs in a President's action, application of the Resolution may be desirable either to legitimize the action and strengthen it by making clear congressional support for the measure or to establish the precedent that the Resolution does apply in such a situation. On the other hand, some may believe it is preferable to leave the President more flexibility of action than is possible under the Resolution. Or some may not wish to have a formal vote on either the issue of applying the Resolution or the merits of utilizing Armed Forces in that case. If Congress does not concur in an action taken by a President, the Resolution offers a way to terminate it.

A longer-term issue is whether the War Powers Resolution is working or should be amended. Some contend that it has been effective in moderating the President's response to crisis situations because of his awareness that certain actions would trigger its reporting and legislative veto provisions. Or they suggest that it could be effective if the President would comply fully or Congress would invoke its provisions. Others believe it is not accomplishing its objectives and suggest various changes. Some have proposed that the Resolution return to the original Senate-passed version, which would enumerate circumstances in which the President needed no congressional authorization for use of Armed Forces (namely to respond to or forestall an armed attack against the United States or its forces or to protect U.S. citizens while evacuating them) but prohibit any other use or any permissible use for more than 30 days unless authorized by Congress. Others would replace the automatic requirement for withdrawal of troops after 60 days with expedited procedures for a joint resolution authorizing the action or requiring disengagement. Still others would repeal the Resolution on grounds that it restricts the President's effectiveness in foreign policy or is unconstitutional.

Several Members have suggested establishing a consultative group to meet with the President when military action is being considered. Senators Byrd, Nunn, Warner, and Mitchell introduced S.J.Res. 323 in 1988 and S. 2 in 1989 to establish a permanent consultation group of 18 Members consisting of the leadership and the ranking and minority Members of the Committees on Foreign Relations, Armed Services, and Intelligence. The bill would permit an initial consultative process to be limited to a core group of six Members—the majority and minority leaders of both chambers plus the Speaker of the House and President pro tempore of the Senate. On October 28, 1993, House Foreign Affairs Chairman Lee Hamilton introduced H.R. 3405 to establish a congressional consultative group equivalent to the National Security Council. No action was taken on this proposal.

Thus far, however, executive branch officials and congressional leaders, who themselves have varying opinions, have been unable to find mutually acceptable changes in the War Powers Resolution. President Clinton, in Presidential Decision Directive 25 signed May 3, 1994, supported legislation to amend the Resolution along the lines of the Mitchell, Nunn, Byrd, and Warner proposal of 1989, to establish a consultative mechanism and also eliminate the 60-day withdrawal provisions. Although many agreed on the consultation group, supporters of the legislation contended the time limit had been the main flaw in the War Powers Resolution, whereas opponents contended the time limit provided the teeth of the Resolution. The difficulty of reaching consensus in Congress on what action to take is reflected in the fact that in the 104th Congress, only one measure, S. 5, introduced January 4, 1995, by then Majority Leader Dole was the subject of a hearing. S. 5, if enacted, would have repealed most of the existing War Powers Resolution. An effort to repeal most of the War Powers Resolution in the House on June 7, 1995, through an amendment to the Foreign Assistance and State Department Authorization Act for FY1996-97 (H.R. 1561) by Representative Hyde, failed (201-217). Other than these instances, no other War Powers related legislation was even considered during the 104th Congress.

On March 18, 1998, the House defeated H.Con.Res. 227, a resolution that would have directed the President, pursuant to Section 5(c) of the War Powers Resolution, to remove United States Armed Forces from the Republic of Bosnia and Herzegovina (H.Rept. 105-442). It was the hope of Representative Tom Campbell, its sponsor, that passage of the resolution could lead to a court case that would address the constitutionality of the War Powers Resolution. On March 31, 1998, the House passed a Supplemental Appropriations bill (H.R. 3579) that would ban use of funds for conduct of offensive operations against Iraq, unless such operations were specifically authorized by law. This provision was dropped in the conference with the Senate. On June 24, 1998, the House passed H.R. 4103, the Defense Department Appropriations bill for FY1999, with a provision by Representative Skaggs that banned the use of funds appropriated or otherwise made available by this act "to initiate or conduct offensive military operations by United States Armed

Forces except in accordance with the war powers clause of the Constitution (Article 1, Section 8), which vests in Congress the power to declare and authorize war and to take certain specified, related actions." The Skaggs provision was stricken by the House-Senate conference committee on H.R. 4103. No further War Powers-related actions were taken by Congress by the adjournment of the 105th Congress.

During the 106th Congress, efforts were made to force the President to seek congressional authority for military operations in Kosovo, leading to votes in the House and Senate on that issue. Subsequently, Representative Tom Campbell and others sued the President in Federal Court in an effort to clarify congressional-executive authority in this area. A Federal District Court and an Appeals Court refused to decide the case on the merits, instead holding that the plaintiffs lacked standing to sue. On October 2, 2000, the United States Supreme Court let stand the holding of the U.S. Appeals Court.[1]

During the first session of the 107th Congress, the Congress passed S.J.Res. 23, on September 14, 2001, in the wake of the terrorist attacks against the World Trade Center in New York City, and the Pentagon building in Arlington, VA. This legislation, titled the "Authorization for Use of Military Force," passed the Senate by a vote of 98-0; the House of Representatives passed it by a vote of 420-1. This joint resolution authorizes the President "to use all necessary and appropriate force against those nations, organizations, or persons he determines planned, authorized, committed, or aided the terrorist attacks that occurred on September 11, 2001, or harbored such organizations or persons, in order to prevent any future acts of international terrorism against the United States by such nations, organizations or persons." Congress further declared in the joint resolution that "Consistent with section 8(a)(1) of the War Powers resolution," the above language is "intended to constitute specific statutory authorization within the meaning of section 5(b) the War Powers Resolution." S.J.Res. 23 further stated that "Nothing in this resolution supersedes any requirement of the War Powers Resolution." President George W. Bush signed S.J.Res. 23 into law on September 18, 2001 (P.L. 107-40, 115 Stat. 224).[2]

During the second session of the 107th Congress, the Congress passed H.J.Res. 114, the Authorization for the Use of Force Against Iraq Resolution of 2002 (P.L. 107-243). On October 16, 2002, President Bush signed this legislation into law. This statute authorizes the President to use the Armed Forces of the United States

> as he determines to be necessary and appropriate in order to (1) defend the national security of the United States against the continuing threat posed by Iraq; and (2) enforce all relevant United Nations Security Council resolutions regarding Iraq.

Prior to using force under this statute the President is required to communicate to Congress his determination that the use of diplomatic and other peaceful means will not "adequately protect the United States ... or ... lead to enforcement of all relevant United Nations Security Council resolutions" and that the use of force is "consistent" with the battle against terrorism. The statute also stipulates that it is "intended to constitute specific statutory authorization within the meaning of section 5(b) of the War Powers Resolution." It further requires the President to make periodic reports to Congress "on matters relevant to this joint resolution." Finally, the statute expresses

---

[1] *Campbell v. Clinton*, 52 F. Supp. 2d 34 (D.D.C. 1999), *aff'd*, 203 F.3d 19 (D.C. Cir. 2000), *cert. denied*, 531 U.S. 815 (2000).

[2] For details relating to enactment of this authority, see CRS Report RS22357, *Authorization for Use of Military Force in Response to the 9/11 Attacks (P.L. 107-40): Legislative History*, by Richard F. Grimmett.

Congress's "support" for the efforts of the President to obtain "prompt and decisive action by the Security Council" to enforce Iraq's compliance with all relevant Security Council resolutions.

P.L. 107-243 clearly confers broad authority on the President to use force. The authority granted is *not limited* to the implementation of *previously adopted* Security Council resolutions concerning Iraq but includes "all relevant ... resolutions." Thus, it appears to incorporate resolutions concerning Iraq that may be adopted by the Security Council in the future as well as those already adopted. The authority also appears to extend beyond compelling Iraq's disarmament to implementing the full range of concerns expressed in those resolutions. The President's exercise of the authority granted is *not* dependent upon a finding that Iraq was complicit in the attacks of September 11, 2001. Moreover, the authority conferred can be used for the purpose of defending "the national security of the United States against the continuing threat posed by Iraq." On March 19, 2003, President Bush used the authority granted in P.L. 107-243 by launching a military attack against Iraq. The President continues to use that authority for ongoing military operations in Iraq.

Author Contact Information

Richard F. Grimmett
Specialist in International Security
rgrimmett@crs.loc.gov, 7-7675